13

Folksongs from Africa

selected and arranged by

MALCOLM FLOYD

226

© 1991 by Faber Music Ltd
First published in 1991 by Faber Music Ltd
3 Queen Square London WC1N 3AU
Illustrations © 1991 by John Levers
Cover illustration by Angela Dundee
© 1991 by Faber Music Ltd
Music processed by Silverfen Ltd
Printed in England

ISBN 0 571 51230 5

FABER *ff* MUSIC

Preface

Africa is a vast continent of many nations, and this collection offers a taste of the great variety of traditional music to be found there. Included are songs from nine different countries, with a particular emphasis on Kenya – one of the few countries inhabited by all three of Africa's great language families. The variety of music within just this one country helps us to understand the great diversity of Africa's musical culture.

Folksongs from Africa therefore brings together a wide variety of music touching on many aspects of African life. The songs fall into six categories:

Lullabies The first music we hear is while we are still babies. In Africa, everyone knows many songs to encourage babies to sleep. As soon as children are old enough to look after their baby brothers and sisters this becomes an important part of their duties in the home. Many African lullabies end up with the baby being offered lots of things if only it will go to sleep, and trouble if it won't – a feature common to nearly all lullabies (think of *Rock-a-bye baby* and *Hush little baby*). Babies are very important to everyone in Africa. They are real riches, when things like food and water can so easily disappear.

Songs for children Children all over the world learn through singing. African children learn how to behave as adults, to dance, to cope with new and strange situations, to work, to count and, of course, to enjoy themselves! The songs in this section are all based on real life around African children and incidents that actually happened. When singing these songs, try to imagine the African situation: an isolated village, probably in a dry land that needs constant hard work. But on no account forget the child's sense of fun! Many of the songs are very simple and should be sung energetically. If you use accompaniment keep that lively too.

Songs of work There is no easy work in traditional Africa. When the harvest comes, happiness and parties are well-deserved. As a cattle herd grows, there is tremendous pride of ownership. Work songs are sung to make work easier, to rejoice in the results of hard labour, and sometimes to make life, with all its rigours, bearable.

Songs of war The four war songs display the encouragement to bravery and heroism that almost all African peoples have sung when demanding victory from their warriors.

Songs to praise There is a long African tradition of praising the famous and important. In West Africa, the Griots are professional praise-singers, while in the East the Nilotics have produced many improvisers of songs to please any praise-worthy figure.

Farewell The last song serves as a reminder that every part of life has its appropriate music in Africa. A new birth is welcomed with songs, and when someone leaves to travel far away, their departure is also accompanied by singing.

Performance

The African words have been provided wherever possible, and should be pronounced phonetically. 'Ng', which often begins a word, should be pronounced as in *sing*. A little background is provided for each song, along with percussion and other instrumental suggestions. It is hoped that you will use these as a starting point for your own ideas, and develop them with any available instruments – feel free to experiment!

Malcolm Floyd

Further reading

1. Introductions to African music: Francis Bebey *African Music; A People's Art* (Westport, 1975). John Miller Chernoff *African Rhythm and African Sensibility* (Chicago and London, 1979). Malcolm Floyd *Music Makers* (Nairobi, 1985). J H Kwabena Nketia *The Music of Africa* (London, 1979).

2. African stories: Ulli Beier (ed) *The Origin of Life and Death* (London, 1966). John S Mbiti *Akamba Stories* (Oxford and Nairobi, 1983).

3. Useful resources: Eric O Ayisi *An Introduction to the Study of African Culture* (London, 1979). Ruth Finnegan *Oral Literature in Africa* (Nairobi, 1976). Taban lo Liyong (ed) *Popular Culture of East Africa* (Nairobi, 1972). B M Lusweti *The Hyena and the Rock* (London, 1974)

Contents

Mwana wange

Quiet and gentle

Sleep now my child, rest your wea - ry head. Sun - light is
Mwa - na wa - nge, we - si - ri - ki - re. Kye - na - lya -

gone, dark - ness is here a - gain. Rest, rest while your poor
-ko na - ku - te - re - ke - ra. Baa! A - ka - li - ga

fa - ther works on. on. _____ Back, _____ the herds,
ka - nwya ta - ba. ba. _____ Tu - lo _____ tu - lo

rest - ing in their pens. Sleep now my dear child, all the hurts of
kwa - to - mwa - na Bwo - to - mo - kwa - ta ng'o - li mu - lo -

day are gone. Sleep and dream of all that you love, sleep and dream in
-go. Wa - vu - vu - mi - ra le - ko - ku - li - r'O - mwa - na ye - ba -

hap - pi - ness, smile u - pon your kind mo - ther's face, sleep my child in peace.
-ke, Wa - vu - vu - mi - ra so - me - ki - ta - b'O - mwa - na ye - ba - ke.

This lullaby is sung by the Buganda people in Uganda.

Percussion ideas:

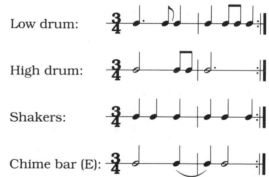

Low drum:

High drum:

Shakers:

Chime bar (E):

These rhythms actually come from the Ewe people in Ghana. They combine very well, however, with this Buganda lullaby. The players and singers should sway in time with the music. You could make up a slow graceful dance based on mothers rocking their babies to sleep.

—1—

Yoo, yoo

This is a beautiful, gentle song from the Pokot in Kenya. It is guaranteed to send to sleep all but the most naughty babies!

Additional verses for the English version:

2. Yoo, yoo,
   Children won't sleep,
   Love them but your
      children won't sleep.

3. Yoo, yoo,
   Children won't sleep,
   Hug them but your
      children won't sleep.

4. Yoo, yoo,
   Children won't sleep,
   Smack them but your
      children won't sleep.

Percussion ideas:

Low drum:

Alto glockenspiel or
Chime bars (F & A; G & B♭):

*'Yoo, yoo' is pronounced 'Yo, yo'.

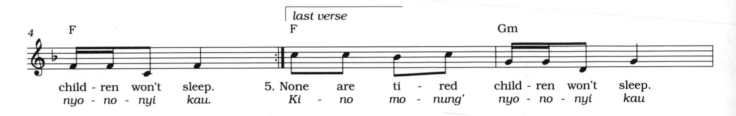

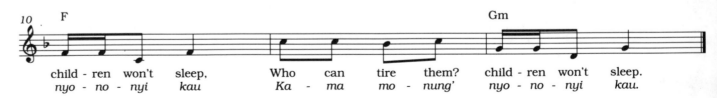

—2—

Little one mine

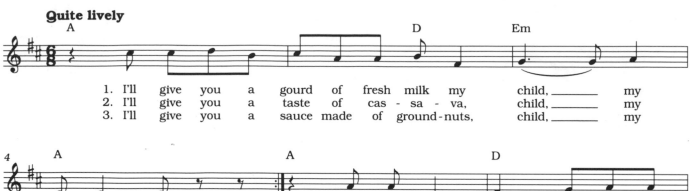

Quite lively

1. I'll give you a gourd of fresh milk my child, _____ my
2. I'll give you a taste of cas - sa - va, child, _____ my
3. I'll give you a sauce made of ground-nuts, child, _____ my

lit - tle one.   4. If you won't sleep, lit - tle one
lit - tle one.
lit - tle one.

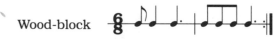

mine,   no - one can make you, lit - tle one mine.

This is sung by the Ga people of Ghana. Try making up some more verses to fit between verse 3 and verse 4.

This song should be sung very simply. At the end it sounds as if the baby-minder has given up trying to get the baby to sleep – but no-one really minds!

Percussion ideas:

Wood-block

Alto xylophone (played quietly)

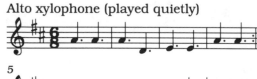

Ayo ay

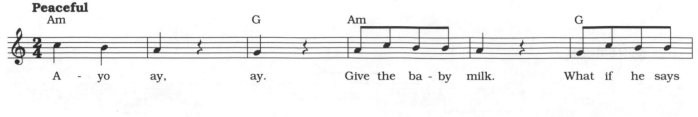

Peaceful

A - yo ay, ay. Give the ba - by milk. What if he says

no? Give him to the maid. Ay - o Ay - o ay.

A - yo ay. What if he says no? Give him to his ma. But

This is a lullaby from Senegal. At the end, the singer is getting desperate! Usually a young girl is left to look after the baby, and she may be worried that her parents will not be happy if they come back and find the baby still awake. 'Ayo ay' is pronounced 'eye-o, eye'.

what if he says no? A - yo ay, a - yo ay, ay.

Can he say no? Give him to his pa. What if he says no?

Percussion ideas:

Shaker:

Tambourine:
(very gently)

Recorder and soprano glockenspiel (tune)

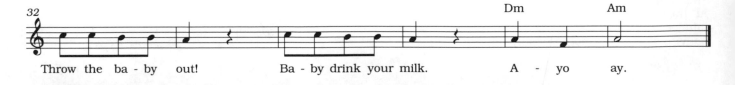

Throw the ba - by out! Ba - by drink your milk. A - yo ay.

Mokong'ondi

Lively

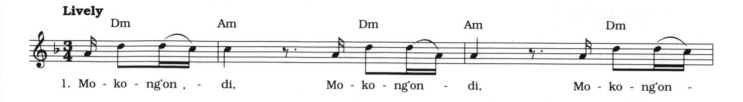

1. Mo - ko - ng'on - di,   Mo - ko - ng'on - di,   Mo - ko - ng'on -

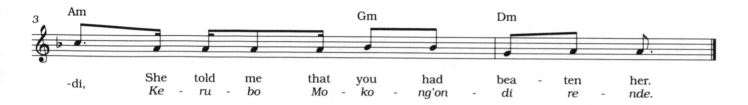

-di,   She   told   me   that   you   had   bea - ten   her.
Ke - ru - bo   Mo - ko - ng'on - di   re - nde.

2. It was not me (×3)
I only told her to go away.

3. Mokong'ondi (×3)
She told me that you ate all her food.

4. It was not me (×3)
She gobbled the food up by herself.

2.*Ng'ai kware (×3)
Kero mwana koyia rende.

3. Noo ñare (×3)
Kero mwana koyia rende.

*'Ng' should be pronounced as in sing.

Kisii children from Kenya sing this song.

Make up a game to go with it, with two groups of children, who take it in turns to accuse each other. 'Mokong'ondi' means 'wife of Ong'ondi'. Other names may of course be used!

Percussion ideas:

Low drum:

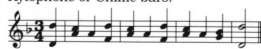

Xylophone or Chime bars:

Kaiyeu nanu

Most children in Kenya go to boarding schools, and some children find it difficult to leave home.

This song comes from the Maasai of Kenya, and is very touching. Sing it simply, and not too loudly.

Percussion ideas:

Tambourine:

High drum:

Not too fast

Send me a let - ter, Ma - ma, from you, from
Kai - yeu na - nu em - - - pa - lai ma - ma, ma -

you, though I am learn - ing, Ma - ma, at
-ma Kai - yeu na - nu em - - - pa - lai ma -

school, I miss you and want to be back with you.
-ma, ma - ma kai - - - yeu na - nu em - pa - lai.

Dance while the music sings to you

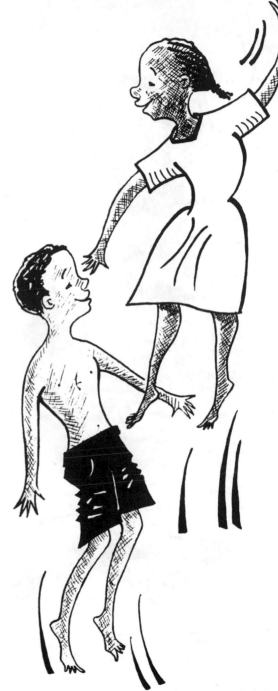

With a swing

1. Dance while the mu - sic sings to you.   Make your - self strong.
2. Dance while the mu - sic sings to you.   Leap ve - ry high.

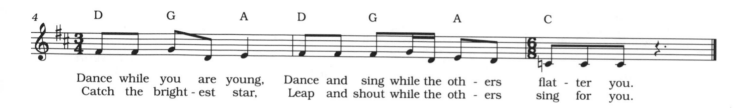

Dance while you are young,   Dance and sing while the oth - ers   flat - ter you.
Catch the bright - est star,   Leap and shout while the oth - ers   sing for you.

This is a very bright and energetic song from Sierra Leone.

Make up a jumping dance to go with it. The one who jumps highest gets the prize.

Percussion ideas:

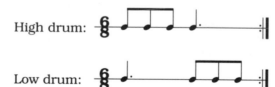

High drum:

Low drum:

Wakarathe

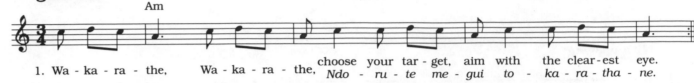

Quite fast

Am

1. Wa - ka - ra - the, Wa - ka - ra - the, choose your tar - get, aim with the clear - est eye.
Ndo - ru - te me - gui to - ka - ra - tha - ne.

2. If I am beat, (×2)
   I'll prepare the meat. (×2)

3. I'll take the meat, (×2)
   To the blacksmith,
   And he will make a knife.

4. The knife cuts clouds, (×2)
   And the rain will come. (×2)

5. The grass will grow, (×2)
   And the calf will eat. (×2)

6. And with the calf, (×2)
   I will buy a wife,
   Who will make us gruel.

7. And all the gruel, (×2)
   Will be drunk by us. (×2)

2. *Nawandatha, (×2)*
   Ngagothejera. (×2)

3. *Nayo nyeki, (×2)*
   Ikarera njao. (×2)

4. *Nake moka, (×2)*
   Agakia oshoro. (×2)

5. *Natuo tohio, (×2)*
   Torore igoro. (×2)

This is a song from the Kikuyu of Kenya, where it is very well-known and popular. It is sung with a game a bit like the British game "One Potato, Two Potato". 'Wakarathe' is if course a boy's name.

Harmony:
Try experimenting with an A minor chord, spread out in different ways.

Percussion ideas:

Drum:

Shaker:

Tuned percussion:

Oteng' teng'

Steady

The creep - - er hol - ding on, hol - ding on,
O - teng' teng' ma - lu - ro ma - lu - ro

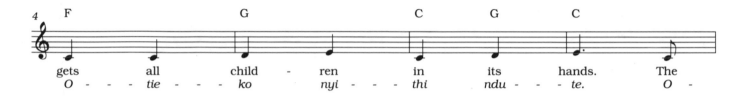

gets all child - ren in its hands. The
O - - tie - - ko nyi - - - thi ndu - - te. O -

creep - - er hol - ding on, hol - ding on,
-teng' teng' ma - lu - ro ma - lu - ro

gets all child - - ren in its hands.
O - - tie - - ko nyi - - - thi ndu - - te.

Oteng' is the word for 'creeper' in the language of the Luo of Kenya. This is a very simple song. While you are singing it you form a long line and the 'creeper' weaves its way around the classroom, or outside.

Percussion ideas:

Shaker:

Tuned percussion:

Jibuli, Jibuli

This song is from Tanzania. It is sung by the Arimi people. Try jumping like a hare in time with the music.

Percussion ideas:

Drum:

Tambourine:

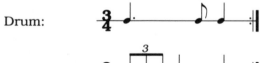

Ji – bu – li, Ji – bu – li, ____ cha – sing the bree – zes,
hu – i si – ning' – i

see him hop – ping high, no – one can catch him,
we – ndye ku – o – ga hu – i ki – ra – – mbo

Hop a – long be – hind him Ji – bu – li quick thin – ker
'Ra – mbo ra mu – ti – ki hu – i ra mu – ng'ko – nje

Run from those who'd eat you, Ji – bu – li fine fel – low.
Ng'ku – mbi – ka – mu – kwa – ta hu – i ki – da – bwa – si.

Abot Tangewuo

Steady

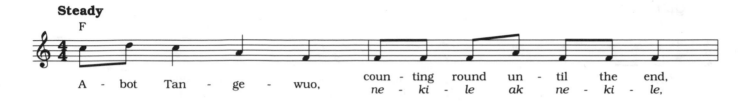

A – bot Tan – ge – wuo, coun – ting round un – til the end,
ne – ki – le ak ne – ki – le,

1 2 3 4 5 6 7 8 9 10,
Tan – ge – be ge – be mu – cho, Ngu – ngo – ro

Put your leg be – hind your back, start a – gain. stop!
ma – nya – ta chu – mbo le – co su – be cha. stop!

Kipsigis children in Kenya sing this song as a counting game. Sit in a circle with your legs stretched out. Count round the legs with the numbers in the song. If your leg is touched on 'ten', tuck it up under you. If your second leg is touched, you must run away from all the other players. Abot Tangewuo is a man's name.

Percussion ideas:

High drum:

Low drum:

Finish with a loud crash on the last note – damp immediately!

Nanu, nanu

Nanu is a nonsense word, used to give rhythm in work songs, and could be sung in place of 'sowing I go, I go to sow'.

This work song from Ethiopia shows the importance of farming, even for children. If the land is not worked properly at every suitable time, drought and famine become more likely.

Kitiezo is a sort of wild vegetable.

Quite fast

1. Give me some beans I can sow, Sow - ing I go, ___
2. If there were no kit - ie - zo, Sow - ing I go, ___
3. When you have meat you can smile, Sow - ing I go, ___

___ I go to sow, Mo - ther give me beans.
___ I go to sow, Fa - mine would have killed.
___ I go to sow, Grind - ing with a smile.

Percussion ideas:

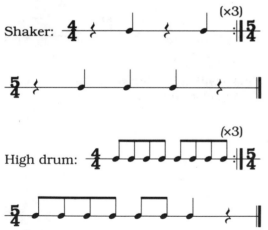

Shaker:

High drum:

Majolo me mabo yinka

Very steady

1. Wa - ter has gone from the vil - - - - - lage,
   Ma - jo - lo me ma - bo yi - - - - - nka,

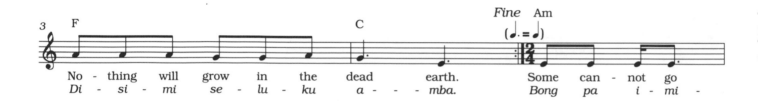

No - thing will grow in the dead earth. Some can - not go
Di - si - mi se - lu - ku a - - - mba. Bong pa i - mi -

-sha - - - lo now, one died, dy - ing, my son.
-sha - - - lo Bong pa si a - - - mba.

Additional verse for English version:

2. Let us all go to find food now,
   Go from this village to chase life,
   No more life for my son,
   Others shall not face death.

This drought song from the Igbo of Nigeria is a picture of life in many parts of Africa. The feelings behind this song are fear, desperation, but also dignity.

Percussion ideas:

High drum:

Low drum:

(both rest in 2/4 section)

Oh ketejo nongusia

Fairly fast

1. Oh, the cat - tle that I bring, I bring for
1. Oh ke - te - jo no - ngu - sia, o - na - -

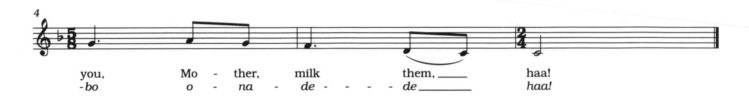

you, Mo - ther, milk them, ____ haa!
-bo o - na - de - - - de ____ haa!

2. Oh, the cattle that I have are
    strong and fat,
    Mother, milk them, haa!

3. Oh, the cattle for my wife,
    perfect will be,
    Mother, milk them, haa!

2. Oh netejo Ipaiyani
    gnabo onapong'o haa!

This song needs no accompaniment of any sort. It should just flow, as if you were speaking it. The *Oh* and *haa* should be very breathy and strong.

The Samburu of Kenya sing this song. They love their cattle very much, more than money, and almost as much as their children!

Yaye yayo

Firm

Ya - yo, fight now, come and fight, ya - ye ya-
Chai - cha - li cha - li - me - no Chai - cha - li

-yo, let them fear our spears. They trem - ble as we ap-proach, they
cha - li - me - no cha - li. A - go - ti nje - ku - tu - myo, Nje-

flee far a - way as we draw near. Raise up your brave heads and shout. O-
-ku - tu - myo wa - re - la cha - li. Ye - ku - gon - za ku - twa - ra Chai-

-ye, ya - yo, ar - rows fly, ya - ye ya - yo, we shall scat - ter them.
-cha - li cha - li - me - no Chai - cha - li cha - li - me - no cha - li.

This war song from the Rtoro people of Uganda uses some strange words. These are often found in African war songs as they are easy to sing loudly and fiercely. Make up you own 'war words' for the whole song.

You could paint your faces and invent a war dance!

The song needs no harmonic accompaniment, only several drums of different pitches continuously playing this menacing rhythm: ♫♫ ♫♫

Nyingunyandenyo

Our land, Kip - te - ber was gi - ven for us to keep.
Nyi - ngu - nyan - de - nyo____ Kip - - - te - ber, ah ha.

Our land, Kip - te - ber was gi - ven for us to keep.
Nyi - ngu - nyan - de - nyo____ Kip - - - te - ber, ah ha.

We must de - fend it from all who come.
Ne - ki - le poi - yot mo - pa - kach ah.

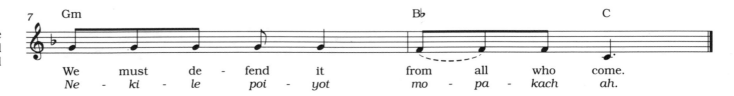

We must de - fend it from all who come.
Ne - ki - le poi - yot mo - pa - kach ah.

2. Arise, we go forth,
    we shall defend our land,
    See the intruders, chase them from here.

2. *Nyingunyan denyo Kipteber, ah ha.*
    Ongepe leye, tugul ah.

The Kalenjin of Kenya sing this song. The second line should be more rhythmic and aggressive than the first line, which should be a smooth melody.

Make up a dance which illustrates the two different moods.

Zira! Zira!

Dramatic

Zi - ra! Zi - ra! The horn has blown, to

war we have been called, for war we have been trained, to

fight brave - ly, to scorn co - wards, to fight to the

end, _____ and we will win! Zi -

-ra! Zi - ra! The horn has called, the

war - ri - ors you see will fight to save you all.

*All chords in this piece preferably without thirds.

This Ethiopian war song must be loud and fearless. There have been many times in Ethiopia's history when it has had to defend itself from intruders. Songs like this must have encouraged many warriors. 'Zira! Zira!' is a war cry.

Percussion ideas:

Xylophone:

Tambourine:

Drum:

Tekele lomeria

2. Warriors prepare for battle
   Ah, ng'aiyeya,
   Ready to defend your homes,
   Ah, ng'aiyeya.
   Ah, ah ng'aiyeya,
   Mm mm ng'aiyeya yo!

This is a marvellous heroic song. Everyone feels brave at the end of it. The Turkana of Kenya have been warriors for generations, and they need to be, as they have been attacked on all sides.

Percussion ideas:

High drum:

Low drum:

E - ne - mies have come to take us,
Te - ke - le lo - me - ri - a_____ Ah _____ ng'ai - ye - ya,

From the north they come and raid,
Te - ke - le lo - me - ri - a Ah _____ ng'ai - ye - ya.

Ah, ah ng'ai - ye - ya, Mm mm ng'ai - ye - ya yo!

'ng' should be pronounced as in si*ng*. The last '*yo!*' should be a fearsome shout.

—18—

Chemworor

Steady

Chem - wo - ror led the Ka - len - jin,
Chem - wo - ror chi - tap Ko - len - jin.

He is the fa - ther of us all, Rich and brave was our
Chem - wo - ror chi - tap Ko - len - jin, Chem - wo - ror chi - tap

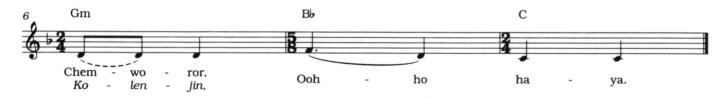

Chem - wo - ror,
Ko - len - jin, Ooh - ho ha - ya.

2. Chemworor's cows have
      curving horns,
   All of the cows belong to him,
   Even the donkeys are his as well,
      Ooh-ho haya.

2. *Aloy pich papo komolen, (×2)*
      Akutung' papo walak
         Ooh-ho haya.

3. *Aloy pich papo sikiroi, (×2)*
      Akutung' papo walak
         Ooh-ho haya.

The Kalenjin of Kenya think of Chemworor as the father of the people. He was a warrior, and a wealthy man.

The regular alternation of $\frac{5}{8}$ and $\frac{2}{4}$ is a striking feature of this song. It may be helpful to count in ♪s.

Percussion ideas:

Tambourine:

Drum:

Sukuru ito

This Kikuyu praise-song has a regular 5 beats in a bar. This is not unusual in Kenya, and if you follow the rhythm of the words you will find it moves along easily. If you use the African words, ignore the repeat in the middle.

Percussion ideas:

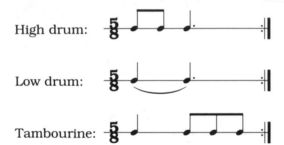

High drum:

Low drum:

Tambourine:

With a lilt

1. When you cough once, drum men dance ma - ny moons for you,
1. *S'ku - ru i - to ne ya tu - mwa - na toi - ri - to,*

Fo - rests freeze in fear, they know your eyes rove all a -
A - ru - ta - mi a - yo ne ma - twen - de - te mu -

-round.
-no.

2. Ten vil - la - ges are bring - ing for your
3. Ten vil - la - ges pre - pare the ho - ney -
2. *To - ru ta - guo gu - tho - ma na kwa -*

throat ba - na - na juice. Ten goats so big and
-brew to soothe your throat, And if your throat should
-ndi - ka kwa - ndi - ka O - na ma - on - do

fat are be - ing slaugh - tered for your throat. 4. So
hurt ten med' - cine men have brought their charms. 3. To -
mai - ngi ta go - ku - ru - ra mbi - cha.

cough, great li - on cough, the mas - ter of the
-ho - ra - ga so - rut Tu - ka - ba - ra - ria

clouds and hea - vens coughs, and rocks will break. ___
mo - go ta - to - kwe - nda ku - mbo - ka. ___

Sing your praise

Steadily and gently

Sing your praise to him who rules all men,

sing your praise to him who owns all cows,

sing your praise to him who fa - thers hun - dreds of chil - dren,

his are the wives with beau - ty, praise him, sing of his po - wer.

This is a beautiful Somali praise-song. The tune must be very smooth and gentle. Make up a verse of your own to praise someone important to you and your community.

Percussion ideas:

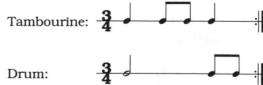

Tambourine:

Drum:

Guitar: Improvise on the E minor chord. Picking will probably give the best effect.

Farewell, my friend

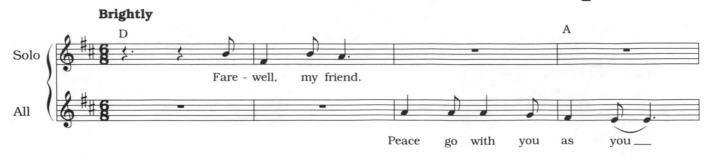

This sort of song is very common throughout Africa. One person starts the song, the others join in as a chorus. This particular song comes from Sierra Leone.

Take it in turns to be the soloist.

Percussion ideas:

Drum:

Tambourine:

—22—